DIARY of a DISASTER
The 1995 Nepalese Mountain Catastrophe

DON JACKLIN

To Diana, Best Wishes,

Don Jacklin

Country Books

Published by Country Books/Ashridge Press
Courtyard Cottage, Little Longstone, Bakewell, Derbyshire DE45 1NN
Tel: 01629 640670   e-mail: dickrichardson@country-books.co.uk   www.countrybooks.biz

ISBN 978-1-910489-53-6

British Library Cataloguing in Publication Data.
A catalogue record for this book is available from the British Library.

This book is dedicated to those poor souls of about
One Hundred and Ten in number who perished during this episode.
So many unknown but still with our heartfelt sympathy and
compassion, are at rest with their Maker. Pax Vobiscum.

Don Jacklin, Dronfield, Derbyshire, October 2017

CAPTIONS
Front Cover: The Green Valley, Khumbu, Nepal.
FACING PAGE: Poster created prior to the event.
BACK COVER: Nepali writing on plain wall.

Printed and bound in England by 4edge Ltd. Hockley, Essex. Tel: 01702 200243

Phoenix Mountaineering Club

Everest Base Camp & Gokyo Lakes 1995

INTRODUCTION

Twenty two long years have elapsed since this event hit the head-lines across the world but as newsworthy stories are continuous, it faded almost as fast as it came in. At the time it was regarded as the worst storm for fifty years in this area which caught us up in this particular place. Since our trek route was a less travelled one , any rescue attempts however belated were directed towards the more populous areas therefore our party and others also caught out had to resort to our own efforts. I have recently looked on the WEB for information and very little is recorded of it. It really is a story which should be told and I feel that our experience puts me in a position to relate the happenings. The Green Valley was at the heart of the snow deluge and from the end of day, 9TH November 1995 until our escape march of the 14TH we were almost helpless. When food and fuel supplies depleted we became hopeless. For such ordinary people such as our team are, this is an epic adventure: for probably all of us the most exciting thing of our whole lives. Jol Pegrum and myself have been on many treks and modest climbs right across the Himalaya but usually good fortune has marked us with trouble-free and satisfying excursions. This one is different and worth telling here in this book along with a representative selection of photographs to illustrate.

LEFT: My passport and ash shafted ice axe kindly loaned to me by my friend Mike Wilde

A STORY OF ADVENTURE, DISASTER AND FORTITUDE
This tale of the trek and fortunes of a group of amateur mountaineers began with a conversation which attracted like minds into a purpose of doing something interesting and worthwhile. Members of the Phoenix Mountaineering club in North England met every month to hike and climb in parts of Britain that held such an interest for us. We all loved our pastime and the outdoors meant a lot to us. "Let's go and have a look at Mount Everest," became the theme especially as some of us were counting the days of having passed the age of fifty and felt that we should achieve something a bit spectacular while we were still able. So the plans were hatched and a small Sheffield company who specialised in organising such treks was paid to deal with the logistics in Nepal. The signees were: Jol Pegrum, Nick Bulmer, Howard Davies, Peter Burton and myself, Don Jacklin. When we arrived in Kathmandu, the principal city and capital of Nepal, the company had attached a young American, Dennis Lassle to our group who turned out to be a competent and likeable fellow who fitted in with our ways and humour very well. Everyone enjoyed his company. Quizzed on why he joined a British group, he was of the opinion that Americans were ripped off as a matter of course whereas Brits were treated fairly and "Normally." We always got on well with our Nepalese companions and had a splendid rapport with them which made all our trips so enjoyable.

Our date for the kick-off was Saturday 29TH October at Gatwick airport: except that when we arrived there it wasn't. The Nepalese Airlines jet was stuck at Frankfurt for repairs and after regular and persistent enquiring it was promised for a 2 hour delay. Then a 4 hour delay. A half day delay and ultimately next day delay! So we toured the delights of the Gatwicks North and South and spent a

night in a Forte Hotel with meals courtesy of the Airline. Chafing at the bit, we eventually set off at 10.30p.m. on the Sunday night. A portent of malfortune? So we met Dennis in Kathmandu where we were all turned away from our pre-booked hotel because it was full. Oh dear, off to an alternative, The Woodlands in Thamel District. Another unexpected change but it was pleasant enough and we were joined there by our designated trek leader, Paul, who whisked us off to the Nepali Kitchen Restaurant for a superb meal and dancing girls in national costume performing classical traditional dance scenes. Very educational. It became even more educational as the beer fuelled evening progressed until Paul decided to impress us with his fire eating trick. This involved the local fire-water spirit, Rakshi. He exhaled a great breath of vapourised liquor across his cigarette lighter and the resultant ball of flame startled the whole congregation whose laundry bill would undoubtably be doubled that night. Soon outside in the cool evening air (very soon actually) we hailed the ever present, lurking cycle rickshaws and three appeared as if by magic. After a short pedalling distance, a verbal rumble erupted about the unfairness of our being carted around by poor Nepalis and we should offer to pedal them as a show of friendship. It was at this point that the race began. In the early hours of a Kathmandu night across an almost deserted town, three Englishmen were furiously thrashing their legs, pedalling Rickshaws in competition to be first to reach The Woodlands with both Nepalis and other trekkers cheering them on. I still feel a twinge of disgrace when I think of this outrageous behaviour but in truth it was good fun. The Rickshaw boys were paid double and after much hand-shaking we left three very bemused faces in the pale light of the lodgings. Madmen!? No, just Brits.

RIGHT: Durbar Square, Kathmandu

LEFT: Flute salesman demonstrating

FACING PAGE: Hindu Holy Man with flute

The people we met in Kathmandu were friendly to a man (woman and child) but as with any community, a mixed bag of individuals. Many street sellers of literally any sort of goods you may desire were constantly around, all hoping for the big sale. I could have purchased a hundred pots of "Tiger Balm," on day one alone! Cafes and restaurants were always acceptably clean and the owners totally polite and welcoming. A few shopkeepers seemed a bit pushy but all revelled in a spell of bartering. I bought some watercolour paintings since they really appealed to me as they had caught the atmosphere of Nepal: I gave a good price for several that I have framed on my wall at home even now. I know nothing of the painter although they are signed, yet for me they are simply a pleasure to look at. One aspect that didn't sit well with me was the begging. As in India it is frowned on by the authorities (maybe even illegal). It is a social problem for the Nepalese yet we hoped our visits there and our spending would eventually cascade down to the less well off.

FACING PAGE: The Holy wheeled Shrine in Bhaktapur
RIGHT: A commercial Elephant on the streets near Bodnath

Wednesday 1st. November everyone arose surprisingly early for breakfast at 8.30a.m. The air was already hot, humid and had that recognisable Kathmandu smell about it, all the scents of the orient intermingled into the distinctly unique odour that I love. It marks Kathmandu as a particularly special place for me and I truly miss it even years later. This day was to be a touristy day. We made for the Great Stupa at Bodnath, my second visit here yet eagerly anticipated. All the shops and artifacts around are an unending source of wonder for their cultural differences. Gift shops, paintings and clothing next to shrines with the ever present Yak butter oil lamps, that pervading aroma. On to Swayambunath, the Temple also known as "The Monkey Temple," due to its inhabitants. And their competitors the Feral dogs. Many a scrap over a morsel of food. Baby monkeys seemingly strapped to their mothers backs never become dislodged even through the rough and tumble. It's a hard life being a baby monkey. "Crafty as a monkey," could have been written here, they are as sharp and as quick as you like; they will whip the lens hood off your camera faster than you can react. The monkeys have become a bit paranoid over the dogs at times and there were some nasty encounters before we left. My enduring memory of this day however, is the sight of Nick wearing a superb Panama hat which he opened from flat packing and wore with elegant aplomb.

Our stroll around the grounds of the Hindu Temple and Ghats at Patupatinath took on a slightly different aspect as we were not allowed inside the sanctuary as non-Hindus. The disposal of bodies at the Ghats I had not seen before and the funeral pyres by the riverside were conducted in a serious ceremonial manner. Often the corpses are not fully burned, when the the pyre subsides the whole lot is pushed reverently into the river, ashes, body parts, carbon, the remains. Local people are truly attuned to this, obviously used to it. Children swim in the river, monkeys swinging across enjoying a freelance pissing contest – what would our health and safety police make of all this? As we ambled our way along the banks back to our taxi the cry from local entrepreneurs was "Cup of Tea Sahib?" Realising where they had just drawn the water from, we politely refused… All such a fascination but back to meet Paul with the task of selecting all necessary hire kit for our impending trek. We actually stayed in our lodgings that night with the expectancy of an early helicopter flight into the hills next morning.

FACING PAGE: Visit to the Bodnath Stupa, Kathmandu

LEFT: Swayanumbath "Monkey Temple," Kathmandu
ABOVE: Nick looking the very essence of
an English gentleman abroad

ABOVE: Hindu tombs with marauding monkey

ABOVE: A funeral pyre on the Ghats at Patupatinath

ABOVE: Jol after being struck by the Helicopter
RIGHT: Jol displaying head wound

Thursday 2ND November. Although presenting ourselves at the airport before 8.00a.m. we did not sit into the aircraft until 11.00. A flight into Lukla airstrip is far less intimidating by helicopter than the fixed wing aircraft even though they are STOL (short take off and landing.) Lukla airstrip is perched on the end of a cliff face and approached through a beautiful tree-lined valley. Approach flight position is vital: the runway is unfeasibly short and the sides are littered with broken aeroplanes. (It always was, between 1993 and 2006 which my experiences included.) So the helibird seemed a softer option. That is, until we all bundled out with cases, bags and all the trek gear thrown after us. Engine still running, it gave a blip and spun round hitting Jol across the top of his head with the boom tail of the machine. Another uncheerful event. Yes, blood everywhere but fortunately Paul was trained to deal with such mishaps so Jol, soon repaired, bravely staggered on.

FACING PAGE LEFT: Monks putting finishing touches to the gateway Stupa
FACING PAGE RIGHT: Resting porters on trek
RIGHT: Almost a high wire act!

ABOVE: A patchwork quilt of a Nepalese homestead
FACING PAGE: The ornate gilded stupa, gateway to Everest

Sherpas and porters come in all shapes and sizes and are truly are the most cheerful and willing of people. Nepalese Sherpas are employed across the whole Himalaya for their dependability and not only in Nepal. But on this trip it was the first time I had seen female Sherpanis included. They seemed so tiny, almost child size but they carried loads nearly as large as the menfolk. I suspect they were light bulk packs rather than the unfeasably heavy burdens that the men hoisted aloft. Often a headband was worn, a kind of sling from the backpack looped across the forehead used as a support. Sounds tortuous but many porters favoured this method. When taking a rest their walking poles doubled as prop to lean the backpacks on thereby relieving the weight from their heads and necks. These people are worth their wages and more. No-one ever hesitates to donate decent post-trek tips.

FACING PAGE: A string bridge en route

At Lukla village, we met our Sherpa Passang, cook Dhambar and guide/sherpa Pemba along with porters and assorted helpers including a few sherpanis. A good crew who made things function well. Shortly after, with all the kit gathered together we set off out of Lukla under the almost completed and beautifully gilded Stupa gateway. With enticing views of massive and stunningly impressive ranges of the Himalaya ahead we stumbled along the trail at first, unable to pay attention to the uneven road. Just couldn't keep from staring at the magnificence. It is like this at first: the sheer scale of things. It certainly is a different world to ours. Great lumps of stone soaring miles high into the heavens, most of it plastered with immovable coatings of snow and ice glistening in the afternoon sunlight. Words don't come easy with this at first. The Himalaya is surely awesome. Beautiful but at the same time inhospitable. We learned to love the high lands but develop a healthy respect for places which do not readily support human existence.

Strange Yak-looking creatures joined the trail and brushed rudely against us walking in the opposite direction. Most of them had their horns sawn down. These were explained as Dzos, a cross between Yaks and cattle, used at lower altitude than the pure bred Yak for transport. Oh yes, they were bad tempered and often fought amongst themselves . The porters told us that the Yaks couldn't live at lower altitiude or their brains would explode. So that was it, Yaks high, Dzos low. There may be some truth in this as a Canadian Doctor told us that Yaks were prone to some kind of Odema if they experienced low air pressure at lower altitude which gave them headaches making them grumpy, eventually violent. We proceeded with caution. Further along the trail we passed by a memorial to an unfortunate Italian who had been gored by a Yak on a narrow path and tossed into the valley below.

So today the shortish afternoon walk ended in darkness at Phakding where we ate in the relative comfort of a timber lodge whilst the tents went up in the grounds. Curried potatoes on the menu was another first for me (but not the last) followed by tea and Hobnobs before turning in quite early. When it gets dark there it is really dark and there isn't much to do really. I do remember getting out of my tent about 3.00a.m. and meeting Pete looking for the same toilet spot. As we stood shivering together for a wee while staring at the wondrous sight of star-filled heavens, a Nepalese voice spoke softly behind us enquiring of our health. It was our night watchman, set over the camp for security. Such peace of mind. Bother those splashes…

Friday 3RD November. Today we trek to Namche Bazaar which is at altitude 11,350 feet above sea level. Slow acclimatisation to altitude gain is considered the safest way and accepted as the norm. The trail to Manju for a lunch stop seemed wearisome but it was lovely to walk by the long ridge of Thamserku covered in fluted snow and ice. Lots of activity along here, many trekkers and porters also supplying local needs at upland villages. Some of the loads carried by these lads are huge, they must be very strong. See the photo of those young men carrying baulks of timber. Portering is a respected profession in uplands such as the Khumbu where it is almost impossible to build roads. It is the age old tradition of transportation: the only means of moving goods around this terrain. Dzos on the suspension bridges made for interesting entertainment. Another saying could have originated here, "Head to Head." Later on, passing by a well laden porter on a swinging rope bridge, I managed to get hit in the eye by a pigs trotter hanging out of a basket cage. No real harm done, just knocked my sunglasses off!

The last linear mile to the township of Namche Bazaar is also one mile of height to climb. In the heat of a sunny afternoon this was a sweaty old trudge for our whole team. Around 3 hours it took before we skipped lightly into the Everest Lodge Hotel where the cook boys were assembling another more than adequate evening meal. Can you believe it? Out in the wilderness it was soup starters this night followed by Chicken Supreme with trimmings! Maybe it was the hot chocolate drinks that helped us to sleep so well.

RIGHT: Porters hauling baulks of timber to highland villages

ABOVE: Namche at night
FACING PAGE: Porters crossing a rope bridge

Saturday 4TH November was decided to be a rest day, a free day to acclimatise and savour the delights of this amazing focal point town on the edge of the now prescribed Sagarmatha National Park. It started off being a small village built into the protection of a natural amphitheatre and looks just like one too. Namche has grown on the back of tourism, trekkers and climbers help to make this place important. There is an awful lot of things to see and do here but what really put the cream on the top was today being market day. This seemed to be something special, not only patronised by the locals and nearby hamlets but traders from Tibet and further areas of Nepal and India who assemble to trade at this magnetic focal point. Such crushing crowds had assembled by lunchtime I could scarcely believe my eyes. Eventually as a relief from the now burgeoning throngs, we decided to hike up to visit Kunde, a smaller settlement over the rim to the North. First we reached the Everest Museum but found it was closed. Perhaps the custodians were patronising the market below. But here we saw our first "Proper," view of Everest which peered at us over the shoulders of neighbouring giants at the head of the long valley ahead. During the ascent to Namche there had been tantalising glimpses in between the trees but here was a clear uninterrupted sight. Nearby we came across a huge stone on which was carved the biggest set of Mani symbols I have seen outside of Tibet. Huge and immovable, the prayer carvings covered the entire surface, it looked spectacular. The Everest View Hotel is also worth a visit at this juncture and mid afternoon tea was purchased while a clearer view of the greatest mountain on earth watched over us. A pleasant chat with our Nepalese companions ensued discussing their life in the high lands. They said that this Hotel had tried to make a commercial effort to attract visitors by flying them directly here to a little landing strip specially constructed for their purposes. It all started off apparently well but critics had already warned of getting to altitude too quickly laying open the fear of illness due to non acclimatisation. Indeed this proved to be the case and a Japanese lady collapsed almost as soon as leaving the aeroplane and could not be revived. The tourist project was abandoned although the hospital at nearby Khunde village welcomed the facility.

FACING PAGE: The amphitheatre village of Namche Bazaar

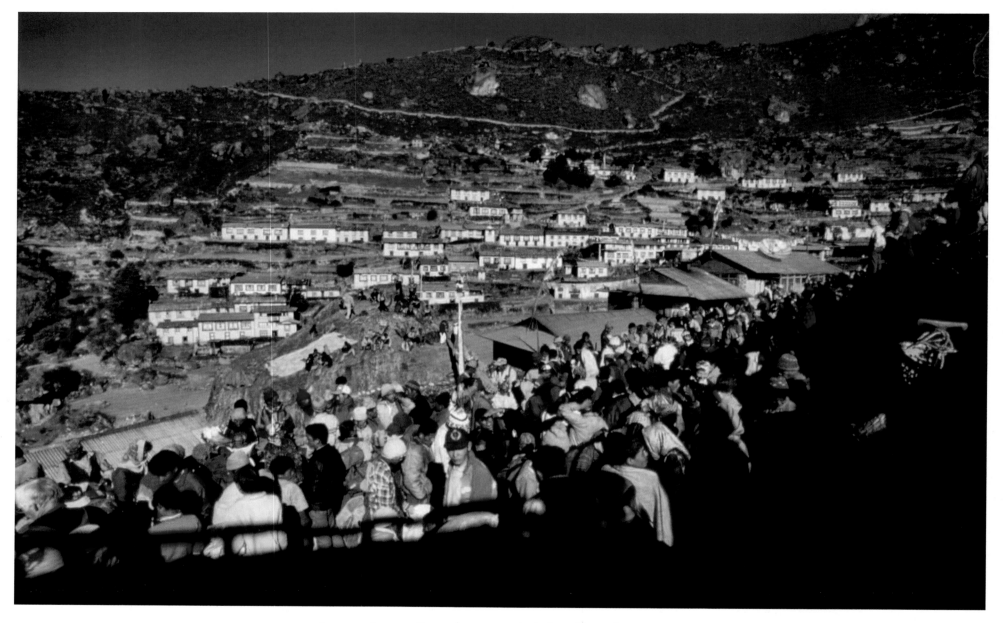

ABOVE: Crowds on market day, Namche
FACING PAGE: First decent view of Everest from the crest above Namche

LEFT: The author in conversation with Dhamba at The Everest View Hotel
FACING PAGE: Khunde village

Afternoon cloud descended on the land as we walked over to Kunde to visit first the charity hospital where a Canadian Doctor was in attendance doing benevolent work. The village itself was a random collection of adobe shelters, housing what seemed to us an impoverished populace. We were unable to discern what supported these people or how they survived in this harsh situation. The day turned colder without sunshine and the dampness began to penetrate our clothing so returning to the sanctuary of the Everest lodge sounded a good idea. At this point we were abandoned by Paul, our English "Leader," who without explanation or reason, said he was off to climb Island Peak with a friend. And left us to it. Someone remarked, "Into the unknown," but neither Jol nor I felt that way. I guess he didn't think we needed him. So be it.

Sunday 5TH November dawned fine and by 7.15a.m. we were ready to leave Namche Bazaar now eerily silent possibly due to the excess of Chang (a local beer brew) consumption by all and sundry.

Paul had gone and Passang our Sirdar was now the man. He certainly rose to the occasion and I for one will always hold him in the greatest respect for his actions and performance during this coming month. It was the same short sharp pull out of Namche as the day before and we began the long hill traverse to Moulo with super mountain scenery all around us and indirectly following the Duhd Kosi (river of milk) along the valley floor a long, long way below us. Our approach to Porte Tenga involved a rare descent – Passang wanted to stop at a scruffy little place but we badgered him into moving further on. There were some excellent photographic opportunities along this Thamserku trail and now we neared the magnificent Ama Dablan as a steady afternoon mist wafted in.

Increasing contact with Dzo and Yak was making us wary and Howard coined the phrase "Yak Attack!" when an impending meeting was likely. Before long the mist rolled in completely and stopped us short by 3.00p.m. to pitch camp. Temperatures dropped alarmingly provoking much fishing about for warm clothing and an early night beckoned. The remoteness was now beginning to be felt: we seemed to be further from civilisation than ever before in our lives. It was exciting and a little unnerving. Or was there something else in the atmosphere? I was my usual cheerful self but I had an unconciable urge to keep looking around me without logical reason. Survival? Nerves? Naw, just curiosity…

The Zoo Keepers Boot. Although our Nepalese team was absolutely wonderful we did have a minor but annoying problem with one of the porters. His personal hygiene was non-existent. He was assigned to be a "Sweeper," that is to say, the very last person in the column to make sure that no-one went astray or became lost. This meant that the laggard of our group was the nearest and invariably within scenting distance: it steadily became a mini competition with us to keep further ahead in the line. Why name him Zoo Keepers boot? Only because it was reckoned that any Zoo Keeper would tread in all animals droppings hence having a distinctive aura. I forget the name of this lad but he was to us, so nice and talkative, quite unaware of the overbearing stench that he emitted. He carried with him for the whole of the time on trek a paraffin Tilley lamp which never, ever worked no matter how much pumping effort went into the thing. It was clearly broken but he never let go of it. Tenacious is the word, amongst others.

Our Cook, Dhamba however, was totally the opposite (we were glad to observe) and quite obsessive over cleanliness. His food prep was immaculate and he even kept a watchful eye on the dishwashers during their unenviable task. As with every trek I've enjoyed with Nepalese cooks I cannot recall any problems with upset digestive systems. Before every single meal all members were ushered to the soap and water before dining. Professionals all.

RIGHT: A carefully balanced cairn by the trail

RIGHT: An assembly of Dzo's with nice horns.
FACING PAGE: The Dhud Kosi (river of milk) and a dodgy bridge

ABOVE: Wayside children look on impassively

Monday 6TH November. Called out at 6.30a.m. barely light, the call of "Bed tea, Sahib," ringing round the camp and crunched across a very frosted ground to the mess tent. The cold was intense but not only that, to our horror, the toilet tent had been dismantled already and on it's way to the next stopover. We never did find out why and who organised that most unsociable act of packing a vital piece of equipment at such a crucial time. Well this did give us an embarrassing problem not only the icy cold but it was a fairly busy site and I swear the other trekkers had knowing smiles on their faces. After a semi warm breakfast we shaved and collected our bits into rucksacks to move off for the days march by 7.30a.m. It was a hard morning across a traverse of a hillside but the excercise warmed us nicely. The trail took us through a strange copse of scrub trees with heavily moss bedecked bark and desperate roots reaching out like demented hands intertwined and trying to grab at our boots. In one sense, slightly unsettling. Spirits of the past? The copse petered out with some very flaky looking bark: it all looked starved of sunlight. Late morning the sun did break through and it felt like luxury. What a simple pleasure, that of being warmed by the sun. It took on an out of proportion sentiment. The pleasure seemed to be magnified : it all depends on the frame of mind I suppose but at the time it felt a real treat.

The trail we now took was not the usual one that leads by The lovely Thangboche Monastery. We did follow that one as our retreat later in the month. Now we were on a lesser trod route heading for the Lakes at Gokyo and broke the journey to lunch at Dole. It was a nice, basic little hamlet well laid out and as we ate we were studied at length by a Nepalese schoolgirl leaning over a dry-stone wall. I've said this before but the locals are just as much interested in us as we are in them. We all like to see something different. Small children just looked at us impassively as we laboured by.

Further climbing to Luza then the trail levelled out as we approached our overnight camp at Phanka, near Machermo. The cloud again tried to swallow us up during the afternoon and being now in a deeper valley, we would lose the sun early. Before we lost sight of it, Mount Machermo took on a grand look of majesty in the late afternoon light, wreathed in swirling cloud and touched with snow. Come on Donny, this is what we came here for! That night turned even colder as our altitude continued to increase. During dinner a heavy frost formed everywhere and we quickly opted for an early night in the relative comfort of our two-man tents and turned in. It had not been a particularly notable day: the surroundings were beautiful of course and we had walked by a field of what appeared to be cottongrass and redthorn bushes glowing prettily. I noted in my trek diary that I was cold in my Snugglepak sleeping bag. Should have chosen a higher grade.

I recall one evening just as we were preparing to turn in for the night, a cold dampish atmosphere just before full darkness took over. There were five or six Sherpanis huddled together pulling their sleeping bags around themselves and one of them emitted a throaty cough. Then repeated with another that sounded like a dog barking. I carried a pack of precautionary throat lozenges with me and in pity, offered one to the sufferer. As I turned away to return to my tent, suddenly there was a chorus of five more coughings: not to be left out, they all wanted a lozenge....

RIGHT: Porter crossing cleared ground near Phanka
FACING PAGE: A cold valley with relieving sunburst appearing

ABOVE: Red berry bushes
FACING PAGE: Machermo in afternoon light with passing cloud

Tuesday 7TH November. A grumpy heap of blokes assembled by the mess tent, bleary eyes after one of the coldest nights I can remember from anytime. Broken sleep through being so cold and with the (loving) attention of feral dogs trying to push under our tent valances for a bit of shelter comfort. I remember waking up to the sensation of a warm body next to me yet not inside my sleeping bag. My wonderment changed to a sort of unexplained resentment and pushed him aside. The audacity. Later I reconsidered and thought maybe we should have shared mutual comfort. What things go through your mind when you are out of your usual comfort zone. Good fortune smiled on us a little as our camp was in view of the sun rising between two peaks and a very welcome warmth spread over us whilst still at breakfast. Indeed the mood of our party lifted noticably and the day's trek began cheerfully as we climbed to contour a minor glacier. As we got higher, habitation became more sparse and I wondered how even these hardy people managed up here? The few houses we passed by were built using more stone than before where wood was the favoured material. Even wood is a scarce commodity in Nepal as there are few spare trees and the cost of timber porterage becomes even higher. Dwellings seemed to be more huddled together perhaps as mutual shelter against the elements than at lower altitudes. Should I have learned my lesson with the feral dog I ask myself? On the final approaches to Gokyo I bagan to flag, a serious lack of energy struck home. I felt quite wretched and even stopped to rest which is not like me at all. Arriving at the lakes camp site I just plonked down and felt bereft of energy. Sirdar must have realised that I was dehydrated but strangely it did not occur to me at the time. As I slumped back against a supporting rock, the cook boys brought me endless mugs of tea and I recall downing at least two litres of cold water also. What a change that brought about: after an hour I was alive again and suddenly began to appreciate the most delectable scenery that I beheld. The Gokyo lakes should be a "Must see," for all mountain lovers or photographers. A few years earlier in the Swiss Alps, a fellow mountaineer from Australia had been here and said the same thing to me. Go see. And now the full reality of Gokyo was staring me in the face. If ever a wilderness landscape could bring on tears of happiness, then this is it. Believe me, it is beautiful almost beyond description. I hope my photograph does it justice.

We met here a grizzled old Himalayan traveller who I didn't unfortunately get his name, but there was only a few of us on this route anyway. Across a long table I could barely hear his dulcet tones but he saw my recovery from dehydration and he said "Keep drinking and keep pissing, youth, and tha'l be alreight." I realised he must have been a Derbyshire man with that accent. Down to earth and realistic. Can't beat it. On his way out of camp he proffered another gem of advice. "Never tek a laxative an a sleeping pill at the same time." A cheery wave and he was off : gone but not forgotten.

FACING PAGE: Zookeepers boot with lamp resting by the trail

RIGHT: A narrow track leads up to a stupa beneath Ama Dablan
FACING PAGE: Mani Stones beside the trail

RIGHT: Our first view of the stunning Gokyo Lakes
FACING PAGE: Mutual scrutiny?

The mountain of Goky Ri which was opposite our camp site across the lakes had been discussed at length before our trek even started as we figured it was a tremendous viewpoint from which to see Mount Everest, especially at sunset. The plan had calculated that if we could ascend the 3000 feet to the summit from our lakes camp in two hours, we would be in time to witness this legendary sunset on the worlds highest peak. What a goal, what an achievement that would be! So, timed carefully, four of us set off just after 2.00p.m. Jol, Nick, Dennis our Californian friend and myself now fully recovered and active. Either out of interest or with our safety in mind, Sirdar Passang decided to do the climb with us and two other young Nepali porters joined in also. It was a lovely afternoon and thankfully the clouds which had previously been blowing in during afternoons never happened. Yes, it was a fast and tiring slog but the determination to catch the sunset was overwhelming and drove us on. I did have one mishap. Sitting for a few minutes rest, I wanted to change lenses on my Nikon FM2 and so pulled out of my belt pouch the 24mm and 35mm coupled back to back. Clumsily I dropped them onto my knee and they bounced off down the mountain at great speed. Horror, I could see them disintegrating as they hit every hard rock in sight. Gamely the porters tried to find them but it was a forlorn hope and only a few fragments were recovered. They presented me with a segment of a front mount: it was almost funny but I did appreciate their concern. I lost two useful bits of optical glass but still had a few others which would record in grand detail.

Our ascent of Gokyo Ri was recorded I think by Nick, at two hours and seven minutes and I remember our vantage point with great affection and pride, really. Truly, Everest loomed majestically over to the East of us but all around us was an absolute plethora of Himalayan peaks, a veritable sea of ice bound rockery, all features clearly visible. Talk about chattering monkeys, our little party was so full of excited happiness. Of course we were not the first there by any means but just being there was a magical adrenalin filled experience. Multi coloured Tibetan prayer flags that were ceremoniously draped across the summit cairns made a lovely contrast with the blue layered peaks beyond. Within our allotted time scale the sunset played its visual grandeur over the high land and crept stealthily over the face of Everest. Our plan had come to fruition. Our group fell silent as the last light flitted away from the summits and our sombre descent began in the half light of a Himalayan evening. As it became darker our pace increased in an attempt to return before total darkness. Yet this took us by surprise, no lingering twilight here, we hastened, yet stumbled down the lower slopes by the light from our meagre headtorches and in the unbelievably quick time of threequarters of an hour we were back by the side of the lakes. Into camp for a late dinner, our feelings were so euphoric that words just did not seem enough. Would any other day ever match this?

FACING PAGE: Lakeside reflections, Gokyo Ri

ABOVE: Prayer flags at the summit of Gokyo Ri
FACING PAGE: Mount Everest at sundown from Gokyo Ri

RIGHT: Male Yak on the slopes approaching Cho La (pass)

Wednesday 8TH November. After a really comfortable night with my sleeping bag inside another spare bag for warmth, it was again a bright sunny day in this situation of open country by the lakes. It was so nice I interrupted my breakfast to photograph the setting in bright clear light. Reflections of the snowy mountains in the mirror-like water were so clear thanks to the windless dawn. Intent on reaching the Cho La (pass) we set off to start the crossing of the glacier snout and picked a reasonable path through the messy maze of swamp-like rivulets. Once negotiated, we paused at Thangnak where there was a small tea house. Quite a shock to find such a place in solitary isolation a long way from other habitation. The afternoon was a serious climb to the base camp for Cho La and as we progressed, the scenery took on an even more dramatic appearance: steeper sides closed in on us and our toil became very difficult. Interspersed between vertical rock faces the occasional flat field appeared: cultivated crops of maize in some cases or grass for use as Yak pasture. Little fertile oases in this aggressive environment. We met a large male yak near the summit, a chap of considerable stature who guarded his harem with zealous fervour. A detour around him was a sensible act yet I managed a great picture of him set in the virtiginous grandeur of the Khumbu Himalaya.

Settling into our camp at the bottom of an interesting looking Cho La was a relief from the effort of the arduous day and it was noticeable that temperatures had not fallen so low as the previous few nights even though the altitude was much higher. Tomorrow we realised that we would top out at something like 18,000 feet. That evening we enjoyed the most magnificent sunset you could imagine, my photo shows the spectacular display: little did we know it was the portent of a most incredible disaster to follow. I noted in my diary that I was reading an appropriate book. Tales from the Hills, by Rudyard Kipling.

Thursday 9TH November. From a decent nights sleep we awoke to our first seriously cloudy morning. The thick mist that enveloped us seemed so clammy even at 6.00a.m. A little snow skirling abaft, a group of Himalayan Partridges circled round the breakfast table hoping for pickings. The attempt on the pass started well enough but it was a loose, rock-strewn slope with no defined route and it became a foot picking, floor studied ascent. After a while Pete became immovable. He did not seem to be suffering with altitude sickness but appeared to be quite ill and breathless. What to do in such a situation? Of course we wouldn't leave him! But what can be done: miles from anywhere and no mountain rescue rangers etc. A porter approached Pete from behind and gripping him by his mid-area, lifted him off the ground and carefully put him down again. This was repeated by another porter. We looked on in amazement as we realised that Pete, a bonny fellow of around sixteen stones was being weighed! There followed the astonishing spectacle of the porters, in turn carried Pete to the summit col on their backs! Such strong people, they were not going to let the side down and this was their solution. This act was superb beyond reason and I am full of admiration of them. Thinking of my fatigue a couple of days earlier I wondered if dehydration was also his trouble. I know how bad I had felt and sympathised with him. It was quite an effort for the rest of us to climb at that altitude let alone carrying such a load. As we gathered just below the col, the sherpas had fixed ropes to make sure we got over the iced top without mishap. It saved us donning crampons and as we scrambled over into the Green Valley the snow

Facing page: The spectaular sunset at our camp
on the eve of our ascent of Cho La

which had been hesitant all morning began to fall in earnest.

Little did we know that our troubles were just beginning. The gradual descent of around a thousand feet down into The Green Valley was tricky and uneven and by 1.00p.m. we were already kicking through inches of snowfall or stumbling on unseen loose stuff. We progressed in groups, I with Jol and Dennis, Pete following with porter and sherpa guides to assist him and Howard and Nick bringing up the rear with Passang and the others. By mid afternoon our party drifted into Drangla, a tea house community again in the middle of nowhere. Some of the porters had gone on ahead and erected tents and were settled in the tea house putting the kettle on. Inside the tea house it was a welcome relief from the blustering storm outside so we sat with a delightful lemon tea and a chat with our new hosts, a delightfully happy Tibetan woman with a little child and a grand-dad. By 4.30p.m. Sirdar Passang arrived with the rest of the crew to see the tents already snowbound and collapsing. After an afternoon of choking on the fumes of a yak dung fire and a modest meal, we trooped outside to find the tents wrecked by masses of deep snow. Whoops. Sirdar directed us to what appeared to be a yak barn or a store house but to us it was a refuge and we all collected our bags and huddled together in this stone walled fridge. With our carrymats or Thermarrests spread out we were in bags by 8.00p.m. but not sleeping, just wondering how thing would be. By this time the snow was two or three feet deep and still coming down. An avalanche kicked off in the distance. Uncertainty ruled. Another group of trekkers appeared in the darkness having struggled to reach this sanctuary. Everyone squeezed up and we all wedged ourselved in and hoped for the best. By headtorch I read a little more of Kipling.

RIGHT: Piggybacking Pete up
Cho La
FACING PAGE: Himalayan partridges
around our breakfast table

ABOVE: Start of our ascent of Cho La, Pete being helped by Sherpas
FACING PAGE: Crossing the iced summit of Cho La, Sherpa supervises fixed rope

Group photo after the ascent and crossing the col

Friday 10TH November. Jol was first to get up and out to see how we were fixed. I have a photo of him stood in the doorway grinning in at us. He is stood on about three feet of compressed snow with a huge pile of the stuff behind him. Oh well, someone said, "There goes our jaunt to Lobuche." No-one else knew what to say. Of course our trip to Lobuche and to the main Everest base camp was out of the question. On our front side of the refuge snow depth was about five feet deep and over six feet at the rear. And still snowing like mad! Prospects unknown, the late night incomers were French Alpinists who had some experience of conditions like this and set about organising the removal of heavy snow from roofs and discussion of harbouring supplies etc. But we can't see or walk very far. Snow is piled so high everywhere, we all muck in with snow shovelling and flattening but after several hours it was so tiring and, dammit, it is still snowing heavily. I could hardly believe that another three figures arrived at the refuge, they looked dreadfully fatigued and desperately tried to muscle into the already full to bursting hut. Big George, a Frenchman who lived in Alpine conditions seemed almost at home here, soon intervened and made an orderly arrangement so we could all fit in. Somehow. Where or how these late-comers had been and how they had made their way was a mystery. But here they were and they were alive. They did not speak English and didn't seem interested in communicating so we just thought they were secret Yetis in disguise and left them alone.

As this day wore on, people continued pushing the snow into side heaps and clearing spaces. We tried to make some sense of the situation and consider what to do about it. Interestingly there was a section of snowdrift to one side of the hut that took on a distinct yellow colour which seemed to grow in size during the day. The roof of the toilet tent, a distant feature in the far meadow was so appealing yet so unattainable. Alarmingly by mid afternoon snow levels attained six feet plus in depth in spite of weight settling and, yes, it was still snowing on us. The back of the building now piled up over the roof and then the avalanches began. Quite unnerving yet we seemed to be safe enough where we were. A sombre mood enveloped the whole camp as people retired for the night. Avalanches banged off continually all night long to the point where we almost paid little notice and fell asleep through sheer exhaustion. I had time to devour another two chapters of Kipling.

LEFT: Jol standing in the doorway of our refuge, first morning
FACING PAGE: Scenery from the refuge at Green Valley

Saturday 11TH November. It has stopped snowing at last. Must have petered out during the night leaving a clear blue sky but bitterly cold again. We emerged from our nest to review the set. Not a chance of moving. Sirdar Passang had been discussing with the Alpinists how to force a route through the deep snow: and which way to take. Those of us left behind here decided to try to force a route through to the toilet tent, a savage enterprise to the lonely structure tantalisingly close but isolated in regal splendour. There was no news on Radio Nepal (on our short wave radios) but it was realised that many poor souls would be caught out by this lot. Under conditions such as these, the ordinary Nepali traveller would simply find a wall or fence to sit behind on their haunches and pull a cloak around themselves to keep warm until it blew over. But with such a covering of this depth they may well have suffocated even as they dozed asleep. We came across several Yaks who had succombed to just those conditions, only a few that we saw struggling out of meagre shelter had survived.

With time on my hands, I contemplated the lives and stories of mountaineers from my father's generation and wondered what they would have made of this. A problem for them? Surely not! Just imagine Tilman and Shipton; this would not faze them. They were adventurous and determined to carry out their objectives come what may. Their explorations had limited prior knowledge of any routes or terrain and we are, in many ways, benefitting from their experiences. By comparison our travels are quite forseen and even regularised. We also have the advantage of knowing how the early expeditions were planned by such groups that attempted Everest from Tibet in the 1920s when Nepal was still a closed country. Yet we all share a great love of wilderness places particularly mountainous lands of geological drama. These are enjoyable and humbling situations which I find difficult to fully describe. My feelings waver between awesome fear and admiration of raw beauty. I constantly try to portray how I feel with my camera but often it takes months of sorting afterwards until I recognise the emotion of particular images. This experience in the Green Valley has tuned my sense of value more than ever before: my perception has been sharpened.

FACING PAGE: Sirdar Passang leading the trail breaking team

So, early in the dawn light, Passang affixed Short skis to his knees and set off, plunging forward to flatten the snow into a workable pathway. Behind him pounded the feet of big George Lozat to try to consolidate the line taken by Passang. Behind George were our younger, fitter lads, Nick, Jol and Howard their boots pressing the path into a more walkable state. Step by step, plunge by plunge, Passang must have used a massive amount of energy forging a route in his estimation of the way out. What a hero. Still, great care was needed to walk along this path or wall as it became with much depth of powder snow each side. Any unlucky person slipping off side-ways might well dissappear and have to be searched for to haul out. Best that could be done and in the event proved satifactory. Work on the path progressed but had to be abandoned mid morning for fear of avalanches caused by sun warming ice on the hillsides. We also learned later that our camp site three days previously near Machermo did in fact get avalanched during last night causing the deaths of (I think) thirty Japanese mountaineers. At the reckoning back in Kathmandu we were quoted a total of one hundred and ten deaths (Dead or missing presumed dead) mainly in the Khumbu region but extending as far away as the Annapurna. We considered this a most dreadful event which has been quietly forgotten but means so much to each and every one of us who lived through it. Indeed our trail breaking team returned, worn out, by 10.00a.m. for a well deserved rest. The remaining daylight hours were spent snow shifting, pressing and general wandering around camp before skulking off to bed either in a grumpy or apprehensive mood. My distraction was to read a few chapters of Kipling: there didn't seem to be much else to do....

The whole of the Green Valley settled that night under its mantle of steadily settling white stuff, all brought to us courtesy of a freak storm in the Bay of Bengal which pumped a great quantity of moisture into the atmosphere to be released upon us as height gain obliged a precipitation. As mentioned in the introduction, this occurence happens rarely, in fact not for fifty years has the Khumbu seen anything like it. These things are unpredicatable and quite unforseen. Mankind will have to learn to live with natures ways whenever and whatever happens.

Sunday 12TH November. Another minor change of plan. The road team set off even earlier at 6.00a.m. as George had spotted some ice movement before the return of yesterday. So they returned by 9.00a.m. uncertain about icefalls. Another expression now crept into our vocabulary: "Avalanche Alley." The route out, according to the maps and a good look at the terrain was flanked by mountain-sides piled heavily with snow and ice and this way led directly towards Pheriche, our escape point marker. But it also veered towards a large lake called Cholatse Tso; little was known about it or its exact wherabouts. Passang remarked about its uncertainty, the unknown reiability of its frozen surface etc. There was no cloud at all and the sun shone so hot it was in contradiction to the freezing temperatures in the shade. Perverse. As a diversion to our boredom and widespread misery, the whole assembly agreed to attempt to flatten out a helicopter landing pad and set to work enthusiastically with scraper boards and boots. By the time for our meagre lunch ration there was quite a decent patch made and we tried to make a marker arrow from collected boulders. I stood at the edge of our helipad and wondered if a helicopter could even fly to this height let alone take off again with a load of people. I had misgivings, thinking how futile our efforts. But the psychological effort helped keep things calm. As things turned out we didn't even see a helicopter until near to Pheriche later on. I had to leave our hut at one stage as two of the girls who were with the French party were crying over their plight and were very emotional. I gazed around at our beautiful surroundings yet it was in fact our prison. I mused that

it would have made a splendid tomb. Our release would have to be a walkout in avalanche free time. I did spend a little time photo-graphing our tomb as much a distraction from my thoughts which were beginning to waver somewhat.

Food and fuel for the stoves were diminishing at an alarming rate but no-one wanted to discuss the consequences. A sherpa lad spotted a baby yak nearby, still alive and with a lot of enthusiastic help, it was tugged out of its hole. It was then presented to the Tibetan owners of the lodge and big George who was a butcher by trade, approached, pretending to sharpen his knives. The girls immediately squealed their dissapproval and wouldn't let him kill it for food!

Unknown to us all, Passang had checked out the route again and came to discuss the fact that the trail at the end of "The Alley," had in fact come to an impasse, hovering over some low ground. Not exactly an amphitheatre but having a surrounding of high peaks. Lake Cholatse Tso was bound to be in the bottom, directly in line but with the covering, neither lake nor tracks around could be identified. This area is a lesser known part of the Everest trail and even the Sirdars are not over familiar with the terrain. Passang's report was with his usual optimism but non-committal. Impasse? As darkness fell, so did the temperature: penetratingly cold again, the only place was inside a sleeping bag. In the darkness I could hear the girls crying again and praying for deliverance. I felt inclined to join them.

FACING PAGE:
Pulling a live
baby Yak out of
the snow

LEFT:
The group of
trail breakers
wearily
struggling back

RIGHT:Nick after
a truly
exhausting
trail break

Monday 13TH November The most depressing of days. At last the great dig-out work to reach the besieged toilet tent was achieved to (literal) the relief of all. Toilet rolls changed hands for tidy sums of money and a (fairly) orderly queue formed. Yet we were stuck here with supplies almost consumed including the whole stock purchased from the Tibetan family at the Lodge. Mid morning and the road team returned earlier than expected with bad news and grim expressions on their faces. Their efforts had been in vain, frustrated by awkward and dangerous ground, the track was impassable further on. Gloom settled on us. My trek diary notes; "I am sick of wandering around my pen, looking wistfully beyond the horizon. I still see another refuge in the far distance or rather a high piled snow roof glistening in the sun. We have not had contact with those refugees until today. The digging has been energy sapping only to discover that they too are in a similarly bad plight as we are. I'm now sick of laying on this stone bed, open door, freezing cold trying to write. Staring at the wickerwork ceiling- even the rats have left us to it."

I also recall having a strange dream or spiritual visitation during the night. An old friend of mine Mr. John Bunker had been my college lecturer in the 1960s and our friendship continued on a regular basis after I left the College. He was a Navy Hero from the Second World War and recounted many tales of his very varied career. Before I set off for Nepal, he had been taken into hospital for a minor operation concerning his foot and after a meal, we parted on usual good terms. But as I slept that night, Mr. Bunker came to me and assured me that things would work out alright and I should not worry. Now I asked myself, Why? I couldn't stop thinking about it. I didn't understand the meaning of all this. That is until I arrived home and was informed that he had died in hospital after catching one of those notorious bugs going round at that time. Had his spirit taken the trouble to be with me and offer solace? It has been an odd experience for me and I have thought long and hard during these last twenty some years considering all aspects.

Just before darkness fell we heard shouts from the porters: people had been spotted coming up our trail, fresh figures. Relief all round, it turned out to be brothers of the woman at the Lodge who had come to check for her safety and wellbeing. They had been pushing a route over from Pheriche for three days and coming to a crest overlooking The Green Valley, had crossed our trail and followed it to our refuge. Talk about the Relief of Mafeking!

A quick scan of faces all around showed a palpable relief as realisation struck home. Some just smiled, others such as our Gallic friends, jumped and hugged each other. Chattering conversation, absent for some days, erupted even amongst the porters as we prepared to be released.

FACING PAGE: Toilet tent being relieved after snow settlement

LEFT: At last, a tantalising view of our nearest neighbours (200mm lens)
FACING PAGE: Beautiful light before sunset from our captivity

Tuesday 14TH November. Now the escape route is joined we are up at the crack of dawn to head for the freedom of Pheriche. Upon reaching the more popular Everest route, we discovered it had not been hit quite so hard as we had, perchance seperated by the high range of mountains leading in towards Everest itself. We gathered that up to this point, Kathmandu in particular and the world in general had not fully realised that there was a problem and as we trekked out, downhill in the direction of Dingboche, the first helicopter swished overhead. "Too late," was the cry. The walk out was not going to be straightforward for a lot of the time. As I described earlier, we were walking for stretches on top of an icy wall of a path with drifts of powder snow each side. All being forewarned and with good fortune no accidents occurred. As our trail petered out we discovered the Tibetans link. They must have plunged down a cliff face at this juncture and now we had to do it in reverse. With a lot of slushy melting snow under the influence of a direct burning sun, this point of ascent became muddy and loose, made worse by the continuous passage of a stream of escapees. Some of the little sherpa girls got into difficulties here but were gallantly rescued by Pemba. Another problem arose which had lasting effects, that of snowblindness. None of the Nepalis had sunglasses other than Passang, Pemba and Dhamba. Most of our porters were affected and so were several locals who we came across before we reached our destination. I can't remember who had the idea of silver face masks made out of cooking foil with slits cut for minimal vision but all our porters ended up wearing these. They looked so bizarre but the idea was sheer genius of improvisation. They still needed treatment but not half so bad as full harsh exposure. By lunch time we had reached a hamlet called Thuglia, a tiny place barely warranting a name but, it sported a tea house. Our cook had set up here, as often is the custom in this part of the world and a tea pot simmered gently, music to our tea-starved ears. The French team had left a little earlier than us this morning and were now about to leave Thuglia for the last stretch to Pheriche. Nick had lagged behind and seemed to be flagging. Passang stayed to ensure his safety and moved the rest of us onward as Pheriche was still another two hour march down the trail. Already our spirits had risen and it was obvious even to the untrained ear to detect happiness in voices again. This afternoon the sun was high above us and truly aggressive but it certainly lit up the landscape well. We passed by the melted graves of dead yaks and even a few still alive and struggling to free themselves. Ama Dablan, that magnificent twin headed mountain came into view before our wearisome group trudged into Pheriche before dark. We found the Himalayan Lodge comparitively luxurious. A warm community room with a good stove and a Hurricane lamp for starters. Decent food again and a tidy bunkroom. Nick was sidelined into the hospital but it seemed he was (only!) completely exhausted and lacking food. The consideration of dehydration also came to mind. Yes, we all looked a gaunt, scruffy worn down bunch – when I look at my photo taken by Nick during our Pheriche stay, it says a lot but it makes me wince. Read another tale from Kipling.

FACING PAGE: The walk-out. The picture tells it's own story

LEFT: Setting off to freedom
FACING PAGE: The last bit of our team's dig, too risky to continue

LEFT: A Yak, dead after wallowing in a snow hole
FACING PAGE: My tired and ravaged countenance taken by Nick

Wednesday 15TH November This experience underlines the importance of little things in life which we often take for granted. Just the fact of having a comfortable sleep through the night can mean so much after being deprived. And a super breakfast: if it had been sprouts and jelly it would still have been a delight when the mood is happiness. We now faced our return hack to Lukla but un-deterred, accepted that this was the very purpose of our being here. Due to the disruptions we were all somewhat dissapointed not to have been able to reach Everest base camp although Jol and I had already resolved to revisit the Green Valley and continue to Everest when an appropriate time presented itself. We had enjoyed our excellent viewpoint of Everest from Gokyo Ri so that was satisfaction enough this time. The American Doctor from the hospital called round to talk to Nick about transferring him by helicopter back to hospital in Kathmandu as a cover for getting two dreadfully frostbitten porters away for operations on their hands and feet. They had been discharged from a climbing party (whose names I won't reveal but they were not Brits.) because they had frostbite and couldn't work anymore. Nor would they pay for them to be treated so we would work a humanitarian "Deal." Howard was feeling a bit off the hooks, so he flew out with Nick and their "Friends," not to be seen again until we all reunited in Kathmandu.

So we set off with Passang and the cook Dhamba, just the four of us left, Jol, Pete who had recovered enough to keep going, myself and the indefatigable Dennis. Mainly downhill now but slippery underfoot, less exhausting even doing ice dancing. Still brilliantly sunny but so bitterly air cold. Not deterred we returned by the populous route and close to Ama Dablan for the classic view. Past a few tea houses , over a few suspension bridges and eventually up-hill into Thangboche. My trek diary reads: "Interesting Monastery but not a patch on those in Tibet." Upon reflection maybe that was a harsh remark but it is in such a beautiful setting and that makes up for a lot. It must have been on the edge of the snowstorm because only three feet of snow fell here. Many groups had squidged their way through Thangboche village and it remained a muddy mess: deliciously increased in sticky-ness by the out flow of effluent from lodges on that side of town. We lunched in a nice little tea house (across town) and set off about 3.00p.m. for the long, very long descent to the Duhd Kosi river following a long string of Dzos over. Height lost then height to gain. A leg burning muscle racking ascent to a brand new lovely Lodge named Sanasa, this was 5 Star in Himalayan terms. Adequate kitchen, warm comfortable community room downstairs, two-bed dormitaries upstairs. Yes, real luxury.

LEFT: The pretty but deadly route out of Green Valley

ABOVE: Approaching Thangboche on the way out, note the mess of a track
FACING PAGE: Prayer flags before Thangboche

Thursday 16TH November. The days from now on are less stressful or exciting but the intense pleasure of being here in the Himalaya is so satisfying. Awoke in the comfort of our lodge bedroom and peered out of the window into the pale dawn light. Yes, a real glass window, an item not enjoyed for some time. A chirpy squawking attracted my attention and over to my right was a really brightly coloured Male Himalayan pheasant who strode proudly into view. I had never seen one of these before, the sheer brilliance of his plumage was startling. Another first and memorable encounter.

A steady stroll for us today returning to Namche Bazaar via Phakding. This trail was close under the shade of the Thamserku ridge so the sun made a late appearance. I caught a nice view of the muted shades of the ice fluting with a sunburst popping over the crest. Namche was just a gentle murmur in the evening as we arrived and our stay was in a different hotel, the Thamserku Taki Lodge where we were all interviewed by representatives of the American Government who had taken the trouble to come here from Kathmandu to assess the scale of the problem. They wanted details of our experiences, names and numbers of people particularly U.S. citzens, routes taken etc. We thrust Dennis forward and they eagerly swallowed his story, prompted by our exaggerated remarks about his heroics (?) I hope our little additions didn't throw them too much… Dennis kept giving us strange glances: we bit our lips and kept a straight face. They were the only government reps doing this, no other countries sent agents to check for the safety of their people. It was mainly I suppose to keep the folks back home informed. I think it is a pity that our own government departments don't show such concern for British citizens as our American cousins. We meandered off to shuffle round the souvenir stalls, Jol found a handsome (he said) carved Ganesh, the elephant headed deity, had a couple of beers which tasted strangely bitter after such a length of abstinence and settled for a comfortable sleep. Boring or what? A chapter or two of Kipling helped to keep me in touch with reality…

FACING PAGE: The Thamserku Ridge with morning sunburst

Friday 17TH November. Not a long hack to reach Lukla, being fitter and it was largely downhill, we arrived before lunchtime to witness hundreds of people also fleeing the uncomfortable situation. Slightly miffed, we dropped our gear at the Himalayan Trekking Lodge and accepted that there would not be a prompt exit from here. Even if pushed, the little fleet of helicopters and small STOL planes would take an age to shift this morass of bodies. Some hardy grizzlies set off to walk back even knowing it would take several days march. So we wandered round the village, talked to a few locals and found a few things to photograph.

The afternoon slipped into grey cold wintry weather and as the light levels dimmed we returned to the Lodge: I spent an hour or so reading the last of my Kipling Classic before dinner. Our porters and sherpas were also staying here in Lukla, not going any further, presumably awaiting further trade in trekking work. We realised that this would be our last night together. One clue was the appearance of quite a delivery of Chang, also brewed here and the Rakshi fire-water spirit of Nepali Kitchen fame. Nepalese eyes opened wide, grins spread ear to ear. So the compulsory party ensued. Oh dear, here we go again was whispered round our table. But their exuberant happiness and enthusiastic performing of National Dances just overwhelmed our misgivings. The singing and dancing went on and on, consuming energy and the supplies of grog until they were so unsteady of leg and kept falling over. Then falling asleep. Simple pleasures! Lovely people. The Lodge keeper came up with some bottles of San Miguel at fair prices plus porterage which pleased us until we became as sober as newts.

Saturday 18TH November. Our adventure I feel is drawing to a close. Somehow our Sirdar Passang had convinced the Airport Authorities at Lukla (his cousin, who scheduled what came in and out and who was to get on or off) that we needed to meet a big silver bird for our homeward journey with some urgency and today was our deadline. Even though he got us up at 6.30a.m. we only got away at 1.00p.m. nevertheless we were extremely grateful for this turn of fortune and felt quite sorry for the grim faces of disgruntled trekkers lounging round the airfield. Most had come in here on spec. without a ticket, hoping for a spare seat or two being available but we all had mis-judged the tangle of logistics that the air fleet was trying to cope with. Thank goodness for Passang and his cousin.

The air journey was only about forty five minutes duration and before long we were reunited with our friends Nick and Howard in the Kathmandu Hotel. They had checked on the two porters brought in for hospitalisation and said they were making satisfactory progress although there were to be several digits missing. But they lived to trek another day. After a most delicious hot bath and fresh clothes, our revitalised team assembled for a meeting with a well known Nepali character, Mr. Bikrum Pandey who ran the Trekking Agencies of Nepal. He had learned of our experiences and the humbug we had been through and he seemed truly glad to meet us alive and well. He singled us out as supreme survivors. I looked a bit sideways at this because all the credit should have gone to Passang. Nevertheless he insisted that disasters and casualties are bad news for business. For us, an excellent meal at the Nanglo Chinese style restaurant smoothed over any possible bad publicity. There never was any bad feeling on our part: it was to us an acceptable risk that could happen in the high mountainous lands. Without this sentiment we would never, ever do anything in the mountains at all. As a conclusion we reckoned it had been quite an event. I forget who actually first suggested the commemorative tee shirts. Maybe it was me but after drawing out the designs on a table napkin, by consent approved by all, Howard knew of a place in Kathmandu that could provide the goods on time. So we were all kitted out with the beautifully stitched red and gold lettering on pale blue shirts for three hundred Rupees a garment – wow!

Whilst researching my available information for this compilation, I came across a newspaper cutting which I had been given at the time, from The Mail on Sunday dated November 26TH 1995 and indeed had forgotten that I had saved it. There is a copy printed here which I made with my Sony Alpha 7 that is in regular use nowadays. The paper reports that two British lads, Charles Wright and James Ryan who were trekking the same route as we had done but several days behind us, were held back by the blizzard and prevented from reaching Phanka: which in fact probably saved their lives. Looking at the photograph of them pushing their rucksacks prone and like sledges in front, it seems to indicate soft powder snow of which they were fearful of becoming drowned in. They were the first ones to discover the avalanche situation at Phanka and by the strangest chance, uncovered a two-way radio device to alert the authorities of the calamity. They were decent enough and good enough to furiously dig at the compacted snow, trying to locate any survivors until they were exhausted. Using even dinner plates, the only available tools. Twenty seven victims were recovered within the next few days here. It was within the height range of helicopters at this altitude and this was their means of liberation. I wonder how they are now after the passing years? And what adventures they have enjoyed since…

RIGHT: Wearing my "Survivor," shirt 22 years after the event
FACING PAGE: The 4 that trudged back.
My anxious face is over the handling of my Nikon camera

Avalanche of death

IN the shadow of Everest the avalanche struck. Within seconds, 26 people were dead as hundreds of tons of snow obliterated a remote mountain lodge. Two young Britons, James Ryan and Charles Wright, found themselves stranded in one of the most hostile places on earth. Their journey to Nepal, begun as a youthful adventure, almost cost them their lives earlier this month. Here, James Ryan talks to Catherine Ostler about the moment the two young men thought they were going to die . . . and of how, through their courage, determination and a stroke of luck, they brought help to hundreds facing almost certain death.

'**W**E WERE crossing a desolate glacier 4,000 feet up in the foothills of Everest when we heard the enchanting melody of a flute echoing across the mountain.

To us it was a pleasant, innocuous sound. But it made the experienced trekkers in our party nervous. 'In Nepal,' said one, 'that is an omen of death.'

It was hard to believe we were under any threat that night, as we sat watching the spectacular orange sunset on the crisp snow. To my friend Charles Wright and I this was the trip of a lifetime, the first leg of a world tour after graduating from London University in the summer. But to the Sherpas, there really was danger in the air.

By the next morning their fears proved right. The snows had come in a hard, blinding blizzard. We were in a white out. You could not see the path in front of you, or barely even the compass in your hand. The five of us in our party managed to make it to the shelter of a small mountain hut. There must have been 40 people packed in there, and we remained marooned with them for the next two days as the snow piled up and our rations dwindled to nothing.

In fact it was the snow that saved our lives. For if we had been able to make the progress we had planned, we would have reached a wooden lodge across the valley at Phanka — a lodge which, before we could reach it, was crushed by an avalanche, and in which 26 people were killed.

But we remained trapped in our white prison. Snow fell thick and fast around us and we didn't hear a thing. The whole valley was obliterated in a white blanket of snow. Noise was muffled and it was nearly dark all day.

Finally, with our rations exhausted, we knew we had to get help if we were to survive. A helicopter was our only way out. But to summon one we had to get to a radio. And to find a radio we had to reach civilisation of some kind.

So Charles, myself and three other trekkers — a German, Ziggy, an American, Mike, and Mel, an Australian — made our way across the deep, soft, newly fallen snow towards where we expected to find the Phanka lodge. Still we had no idea of the devastation awaiting us.

EERILY, the disaster was an invisible one. As we approached we assumed that the only reason we could not see the lodge was that snow was banked up over it.

Finally we saw figures standing watching our progress across snow so soft and deep that it threatened at any moment to swallow us up. With 100 yards to go, Charles used his bag as a sledge and all pushed our way across.

Our journey, which normally would have taken 15 minutes, had lasted two-and-a-half hours and when we arrived we were elated. We still had no idea of the tragedy that had taken place. But then we learned from two survivors of the avalanche that a party of Japanese and some Nepalese — 26 people in all — were missing, believed dead. The two Nepalese boys had survived because they were on the roof of the lodge clearing off the snow.

As the avalanche crashed down they were saved because, standing on the roof, they were higher up than those inside. It was only a matter of feet, but it meant that the two boys were covered in a thin layer of snow. Still it had taken them an hour to clamber just ten yards to safety,

SURVIVORS: Charles Wright and James Ryan in the Himalayas

frantically digging their way out. Now, alive but paralysed with shock, they stood rigidly in the snow, barely able even to speak. We knew that we had to dig in search of survivors — we had heard of people surviving for up to three days under avalanches — but the boys, their blank stares unfocused on the dreadful scene, could offer us no help.

We just started digging, using metal dinner plates from our rucksack. It was the only thing we could do. Charles had muttered 'I don't want to see a dead body,' but he knew we had to do it. Just hours before, we had been two 22-year-old men out on an adventure. Up to then our lives had been privileged and sheltered.

We came from happy homes in which we had been cosseted. I don't think either of us had ever wanted for anything. I was the son of a former Yorkshire cricketer

and went to Millfield School. Our family home is a pleasant detached house in the village of Almondbury, near Huddersfield. Charles is from Barnby, Suffolk, where his father farms.

But suddenly we were in the middle of a real crisis, and we had to cope with it alone. I think we both grew up very fast during those terrible hours. At first as we dug we did not know whether we could cope with what we were finding. It was to be the first time either of us had ever encountered death. We were hit by stomach cramps and nausea at the prospect. But as the bodies began to be uncovered — we found only three of the 26-strong party — a strange sort of calm set in. We were even able to look at their frozen faces, distorted with fear and pain in death. As far as we could work out, the incredible force of the avalanche had

RESCUE: The moment Ryan and his companions knew they were safe

obliterated the lodge, dispersing the bodies over 20 yards, buried under tons of snow and rock.

AFTER half an hour of frantic digging my hand touched a leg, two feet down in the snow. I called Charles over and, scrabbling furiously at the snow, we uncovered the body of a Nepalese boy who had been in a kitchen tent beside the hut. Then, close by, we found another body — of a kitchen boy, still clutching a pot.

After maybe another 20 minutes of digging, we came across a third body — of a Japanese man inside the entrance of the wrecked shelter. Beside him, just out of reach of his outstretched hand, was a radio. Miraculously, it was switched on — and

tuned to the emergency channel. We couldn't believe we'd found it. This tiny walkie-talkie was the only means of contact with the outside world in the valley, and we'd come across it in the snow.

We imagined him walking into the lodge clutching it, saying 'Don't worry, we'll be safe with this,' when the avalanche hit. We later discovered that although many more trekkers had been stranded in Nepal's worst avalanche disaster, we were the first to raise the alarm.

We called Himalayan rescue on the radio and begged for a helicopter to airlift us all out, but radio reception was terrible. We could not understand what was being said to us, and we were not sure that a helicopter was on its way. We carried on digging, still hoping there might be someone alive in there, and all the time praying that we would be rescued. But we were exhausted and dehydrated and in the end we gave up, after finding just three bodies.

It was only later, when we had reached safety that we heard there had indeed been a survivor buried in the snow beneath us. He could hear us and had been screaming at us for help, but we could not hear him. He was finally dug out the next day.

We covered the bodies we'd found with snow and marked them with stakes so the Nepalese could find them, and then set about making a flat area for the helicopter to land. We stamped out a five metre circle in the snow and marked it with a large H using ashes.

Every half hour we made another call on the radio. They confirmed a helicopter was on its way, but it could not identify where we were. There are three different

INCHING TO AID: James Ryan's party struggles to the Phanka mountain shelter to seek help, unaware that 26 people lay dead inside   Picture research: LENA KARA

languages spoken in the region and no messages seemed to be getting through.

Finally, after three hours, a helicopter whizzed overhead — but carried on. We couldn't believe it had not spotted us. In fact the pilot had, and after a few minutes he flew back and landed on the spot we had marked in the snow. He must have been a brilliant pilot, because despite the very high winds and the fact that the helicopter sank a foot into the snow, he got us all out of there and to the safety of Lucknaw, the nearest village. Within hours, helicopters were shuttling back and forwards between the disaster area and Lucknaw with other trekkers who had been marooned elsewhere in the snow. In all 300 people were rescued — thanks to the call we were able to make on that dead man's radio.

IT WAS not until three days later, when we reached Kathmandu 190 miles away, that we were able to tell our families all was well. We will never forget hearing Charles bellowing down the phone: 'I'm alive mum, I'm alive, dad, I'm alive!'

It was a huge relief to be in Kathmandu. Until we left the mountains I don't think our ordeal really sank in. In fact it is still hard to believe that we went through all that.

And, despite the danger we had been in, and to our parents' horror, the first thing we did in Kathmandu was to go white water rafting. It may seem strange that we should want to put ourselves in further danger. But we don't see it like that. We were celebrating our survival.

It was great to be alive.'

There is a sequel to this story. The immediate aftermath and subsequent inquest revealed the extent of the troubles which went further than we knew. The great snowfall dumped an unprecedented amount over a large area, from the Khumbu as far as the Annapurna and disrupted the lives of travellers and visitors but it badly affected the general population for the winter months to come. If our party had run out of food and fuel in less than a week then so had everyone else. Hardship is the norm in these mountain regions but it had struck the locals even worse this time. I can find no record of rescue or help for these hill villages in the aftermath. I guess something must have been done about it but nothing seems to have been written down. A recurring thought haunts me concerning those unfortunate Japanese who where killed by avalanche in the place of our camp at Phanka, near Machermo. But for a couple of days that could have been us. I reckon that is a close call and , as the saying goes, "There but for the Grace of God go I." I can only say thank you.

By the year 2000, my good friend Jol Pegrum and I had determined to return to Nepal on our own to retrace the essence of the attempted trip in 1995. This time we would reach Everest base camp and stand on the Kalar Patar ridge to experience sunset on the Great Mountain from that superb viewpoint. This time things went to plan and here follows a summary of events.

Jol and I are totally comfortable with each other on trek. We both like similar things and both thoroughly enjoy the mountain wilderness life. So during year 2000 the flights were booked and we landed in Kathmandu on the 21st October to relish the whole atmosphere of the place. The Kathmandu Guest house provided pleasant accomodation and the Third Eye restaurant most acceptable meals. At first I was not very keen on this variation in my diet but being dragged protesting by Jol, their Lamb Biriani converted me to be an enthusiast. Next day we enjoyed a nostalgic walk around the city and as if by magic, ended up in the Rum Doodle, that most respected and renowned watering hole. Still plastered all over the place were the giant Yeti footprint beer mats with the names of the famous climbers hand written across. Lots of photos pinned about, some curling and fading with age now but an absolutely unique atmosphere. A late evening browse through the delights of Pilgrims bookshop was a pleasure that will never be repeated as I learned later that it burned down in a fire that swept through the Thamel district in May 2013. Oh woe, what a loss. I read on the WEB that there are plans to reopen in another place but the original aura is gone forever.

The following day we awaited our helicopter flight to Lukla with a team of English speaking Russian climbers. A change of plan. Oh crumbs, we thought (or similar such words) here we go again with alterations, meaning probable disasters but this was not the case. Ushered into a little eighteen seater STOL aeroplane we were strapped in by friendly stewardesses who promptly left the aircraft. The Pilot came aboard and turned to greet passengers – a Nepalese female Pilot! One Russian at the back uttered that immortal phrase, "Om Mani Padme Hum," to the consensus of humour from all on board. To her credit, she did make a perfect landing at Lukla, that most scary of airports anywhere and yes, the wreckage of previous crashes were still in evidence at the sides of the strip.

FACING PAGE: Newspaper cutting from the time

ABOVE: A visiting Lama ceremony, Thangboche
FACING PAGE: Thangboche Monastery in it's beautiful setting

For just the two of us with only a modest trek bag each, we engaged a youth named Raj Khumar-Rai as recommended by Chumba, one of our previous trek Sirdars. Our plan was to use the wooden trek lodges en route as a less complicated way for our night stops instead of the need for a camping/cooking team. We managed to be in Namche Bazaar within two days and decided upon a rest day for acclimatising after the famous one mile high for one mile long hack into the amphitheatre of the town. It was comparatively quiet compared to the market day experience of 1995 and we found some interesting people to chat with. None more than a little slip of a girl from Australia who only looked about seven stones. She had descended from Gorak Shep in the one day! We made a shortish trip on a less trod path to the west of Namche and discovered a new-to-us monastery where we were made very welcome by the monks. It proved to be a little more tiring than I expected and next day I began to feel the effort.

It was a while before we located our porter lad. It became a frustrating hunt: he said he was going to visit a relative in the next valley but now he was missing. Occasionally we though he might have legged it and left us adrift but eventually turned up late, wanted paying for his missing day then cleared off again to buy himself a few things. Life is full of compromises. The day wasn't wasted. It was a stiff walk but we made it to Thangboche village that afternoon and settled for a cosy little rat infested hut for the night. The Thangboche Monastery is in a most splendid setting on a raised mound surrounded by wonderful snow capped mountains and Rhodedendron trees. Coloured prayer flags were draped in abundance to celebrate the visit of a senior Lama and a small ceremony was enacted in his honour. It is so pleasant here, the sort of place you don't want to leave except for the antics of the rats in our lodge who were engaged in a ceremony of their own, another freestyle pissing competition whilst running across the bamboo ceiling of our bedroom.

When we moved on next day and passed by Pheriche where we emerged from our captivity in 1995, it all appeared so pleasant and almost summery. This time we checked in at the Himalayan Rescue centre and were offered a check on altitude acclimatisation. Jol was coping much better than I so we decided upon another rest day. This "Rest," day consisted of quite a severe climb up the lateral slopes of the valley leading to Island Peak which we could see and enjoy glistening in the distance. We were to visit what our young porter Raj described as "A wise Lama." This old guy lived halfway up the side of a mountain in a shallow cave having a bit of frontal masonry and a cloth curtain to protect him from the elements. The locals brought him food and drink in exchange for solving problems such as who to marry, when to plant the corn at the most auspicious time or where to bury the mother-in-law. But his dwelling was a fantastic place for photography. New prayer flags in front of his cave looked so beautiful when backlit, surrounding the shining ice mountain in the distance.

Down in the village of Dingboche below the cave, we gently sipped green tea at a small bistro when an American chap ran in from the Island Peak trail in great distress. Help, drama! His friend had fallen unconcious, suspect high altitude sickness. Jol the Hero, trained as a first aider, sprang to the rescue. He collected two poles and a strong blanket to fabricate a stretcher and raced off up the trail with the American and two other Nepalis. A runner was sent down to

Pheriche for the doctor who came as quickly as he could along with a German friend with a Gammow decompression bag. Alas too late, the chap, A big Texan fellow had died of Celebral odema. But not only he, a Canadian Lady on the Northern route and, (a rare happening) a Nepali youth had also succombed to H.A.S. The locals felt the sadness too, several were crying as the stretchers were carried away. There is no rhyme or reason who succombs to H.A.S. or why. The approach symptons are there to be noticed by a companion who must try to take the remedial measures. Best to travel with others and make sure they don't hate you!

RIGHT: Island Peak from the Hermits cave home

Over the next few days the air became thinner, colder but with that harsh sunshine that happens here as we approached much closer to Everest Base Camp. Now I find I am walking much slower and feeling quite tired. Not altitude sickness but later I realised how dehydrated I had become. I later berated myself for not following our own understood procedures. The "Above The Clouds Hotel," was a poor old wooden shed, a veteran of many severe years of Himalayan weather and certainly looked it. But it served our purpose for a couple of nights of refuge. Some ungrateful wretch said it was barely fit for purpose but I noticed he didn't opt to sleep outside in the cold. On Monday 30TH October, we shuffled off for Gorak Shep, the last and highest place on this particular trip. Jol who was in fine form was up early and left before me to try to secure accomodation for our night as we guessed it might be in short supply. I followed later with Raj and used my photography stops as an excuse for stealing several rests. With a bed place set for the night, we all three plodded our way to the Kalar Patar ridge, aiming for a good viewpoint and sat in a row looking straight into the face of Everest. The nearest and clearest view I have had up to that point. This was our goal in 1995 and now we had made it five years later. At that time I was sixty years old and felt quite proud of my-self. Friends said I was foolhardy but what is life all about? If I had not done it I would have fretted away. Fortunately I stayed fit enough to continue trekking in the Himalaya until age sixty five but now I simply enjoy the British hills. And my memories.

Whilst waiting for the sunset, our Raj looked dismayed at all the Tibetan prayer flags strewn all around by the strong winds up there, laid in between rocks or down gullies under our feet. So we spent an hour with him retrieving the fairly new flags, helping him restring them and secure in a prominent position as intended. They looked bright and beautiful. The smile on his face said it all. My bonus was a lovely picture of Mount Pumori framed by an airborne arch of colourful cloth against a blue/black sky. I'm not sure which was the most moving, this or the slow steady encroachment of golden sunset across Everest and together with Lotse and Nuptse gave a pallette range of reds, orange and gold that was joyous to behold. Mission achieved, we wound our way back in the dark to the lodgings, dark, so dark we could not see each other : the light of our little LED headtorches was gobbled up, the blackness so extreme. Torches were not so good in those days. No wonder people go to bed early out there. Our communication was by estimation of each others voices sound distance.

Next morning we went to inspect the mouth of the Khumbu icefall where all the climbers basecamps are sited at the end of a ridge walk from the lakes at Gorak Shep. Usually attempts to the summit of Everest begin here. Enthusiast Jol dived amongst the snowy undulations around the site searching for souvenirs but since a creditable clean-up there were meagre pickings: an old crampon, a ladder rung, a karabiner, an unused Don Whillans knuckleduster...

FACING PAGE: Everest and Nuptse in clear afternoon light

LEFT: Pumo Ri and restrung prayer flags
FACING PAGE: Everest in sunset glow

The last part of this trek was to revisit Drangla in the adjacent Green Valley. Curiosity obliged us to see what the place looked like without six feet of snow covering and on this day, 2ND November, we directed Raj directly down the main trail to Pheriche to lodge us in at the Pumori Hotel whilst we took a branch path that would lead us to the feared Cholatse Tso Lake. In today's strong light the beautiful turquoise water looked absolutely inviting. Drangla made little impression on us. The people were not the same ones as in 1995 so we paid homage, bought a few cups of tea and retired back to the lake. We both remarked how time and memory plays tricks on the mind. But it was perhaps as well we did not pursue our Sirdars extended snow track after all. It would have led us straight onto a delicate lake surface or into a multi torrent of a boulder strewn river, today crashing and angry, barring our way forward. We walked the bank, up and down, scanning for a crossing until in desperation, threw our rucksacks over the narrowest point: thus committed, made olympic sized efforts jumping across.

There is little else to say about this trek. It was a relatively easy, happy walk back via Thangboche, Namche Bazaar and so to fly out of Lukla. We had done what we set out to do, satified the frustrations of the 1995 expedition and for me, I enjoyed the great photography. Also we met a very entertaining couple in the Paradise Restaurant in Thangboche: he was a Dutchman, she a Yugoslav. Both fluent in English and so intelligently humorous they seemed almost out of character. We spent some time with a mixed bunch in Namche, in the only pool room/bar in town. Good company again, Canadian, Mexican and Brits. Two Sheffield achitectural students

homed in on my accent and claimed brotherhood which cost me another few beers. We bade farewell to Raj at Lukla and after the wages were paid we gave him another £20 and a pair of binoculars which he liked as he was always asking to look through them on trek. We were about to discard the box they came in but he urgently seized it. So we guessed they were ultimately to be put up for resale.

And by the 9TH November we were back in the loving embrace of Kathmandu and the fevered atmosphere of the Rum Doodle Bar. Positively glowing with happiness we strolled along to a nice Thai Restaurant and broke more rules by eating a meat dish followed by ice cream.

Friday 10TH November. Payback time for our peccadilloes as we enjoyed the company of the porcelain pony all morning. Our return flight was announced very delayed which gave us time to visit the Monkey Temple again. Hailed a triporteur scooter taxi that proved an exciting journey as it involved the steep hill en route to the back entrance. Down to second gear, down to first gear then the driver got out and ran alongside pushing. Eventually it puffed to a standstill so out we got and pushed the bl—dy thing to the top! Toured around town including the Royal Palace where there was a Royal guard on duty and climbed inside a huge wooden built Pagoda many storeys high and very ancient. It certainly showed it's age needing lots of maintenance, holes in walls, missing floorboards, parts of balconies gone. Nerves calmed by a return match with the Rum Doodle then away, late but happy.

So glad we did this one.

FACING PAGE: Ama Dablan, classic view

LEFT: Cholatse Tso (lake) in clear open glory
FACING PAGE: Imperial guard, old Palace, Kathmandu,
with musket and bayonet

Photographic notes

For years my regular cameras have been Leicas which I still enjoy using. Just prior to embarking on my Himalayan travels I had several climbing accidents (we can't all be Joe Browns) and seriously curtailed the lives of a few valuable Leica reflexes and lenses. Not wishing to repeat this expensive pastime I purchased a pair of Nikon FM2 film bodies and half a dozen lenses after reading the exploits of Galen Rowell. These would prove adequate and no tears would be shed if these "Disposable," instruments came to grief. I had some experience in Britain of battery powered cameras that ceased to work in cold weather conditions so the FM2s were ideal for the frozen climate I intended to visit. Even if the intense cold stopped the little button cells of the exposure meter flowing, the shutters would still be fully usable being of manual mechanical design: settings decided by experience and calculation. In the days before digital capture, film produced very acceptable results and for the most of my work I used Fuji Velvia for its bright colours and Kodachrome for permanence.

The images in this book have been scanned from colour slides, dust cleaned in my computer (after 22 years of repose) a bit of cropping and minor exposure tweaks applied to compensate for a few of my inaccuracies in the field. Exposure in bright snowy weather can be deceptively tricky. I do hope my illustrations convey visual emphasis to the related story.

Don Jacklin, Dronfield, Derbyshire. January 2018

Mini profile.

Don Jacklin was born and raised in Sheffield, South Yorkshire and developed a taste for adventure through the Scout movement and motorcycling which spread the reach of many places hitherto unknown. Having enjoyed a full and varied career in the Heating and Ventilating industry he is now retired and assembling stories of the interesting experiences of life. An active member of the Phoenix Mountaineering Club including a term of President, from 1985 to 2006 and veteran of twenty two treks and climbs mainly in the Himalaya but also Patagonia, the Tien Shan, Tibet and the Karakoram. Successful exhibition of Photographs at Doncaster Museum and Art Gallery 2002 and several winners in National competitions notably 2008 "Wanderlust," annual. He now lives in Dronfield, Derbyshire with wife Elaine who compete in Photography together.

FACING PAGE: The Bodnath Stupa at night from a roof café

Above: My portrait taken atop Pen-y-Fan, Brecon Beacons on my 75TH Birthday (2015)